Ta
Pictures

by Max Bates
illustrated by Rob Hefferan

HOUGHTON MIFFLIN BOSTON

Printed in China

ISBN-13: 978-0-547-02009-9
ISBN-10: 0-547-02009-0

5 6 7 8 9 0940 15 14 13 12 11 10

I see a bug.

I see a tree.

I see a bird.

I see a flower.

I see a skunk!

Responding

TARGET SKILL **Cause and Effect**

In this book, a raccoon takes pictures. Tell one thing that happens in the story. Tell why it happens. Make a chart.

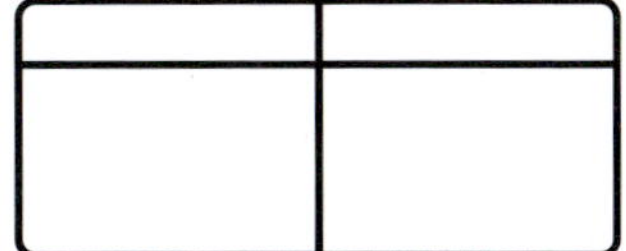

Write About It

Text to Self What if you had your own camera? Draw a picture of a photo you would take outside. Label the things in your picture.

for | **go**

TARGET SKILL **Cause and Effect**

Tell what happens and why.

TARGET STRATEGY **Question**

Ask questions about what you are reading.

GENRE **Fiction** is a story that is made up.